HELP GOD, I AM ANGRY

HELP GOD, I AM ANGRY

CHERYL TRAVIS

MERRILL
PUBLISHING

ISBN: 978-1-950719-24-2 (Hardback)

ISBN: 978-1-950719-25-9 (eBook)

Any references to historical events, real people, or real places are used fictiously. Names, characters, and places are products of the author's imagination.

First printing edition 2019.

J Merrill Publishing, Inc.

434 Hillpine Drive

Columbus, OH 43207

www.JMerrillPublishingInc.com

This book is dedicated to my Mother, Juanita Travis. Mom, I am in awe of your ability to calmly diffuse situations and quietly fight battles. Peace seems to follow you wherever you go. Your calm but very powerful responses to external and internal conflict are amazing to me. You are a silent warrior queen who is beautiful inside and out. Thank you for showing me how to fight using love. Thank you for being an example of what grace looks like. You are the epitome of class. I love you.

INTRODUCTION

Satan attacks and arrests our thoughts. He kills all positive motivation by manipulating our emotions. One of those emotions is Anger. In this book, we will talk about anger, its agenda, and how to conquer it. This book is one in a series of short pocket-books that are designed to assist and support your journey to fulfill God's design and purpose for your life. My prayer is that using the information contained will destroy the emotional roadblocks that we all encounter on our way to realizing victory.

1

ANGER INTRODUCED

I remember growing up in a very loving home. I was fortunate in that I felt protected. There was a sense of unity and bond in my household.

As I grew, I realized I had friends who did not feel that same protection, love, or bond. I also had friends who could be angry with their parents and siblings for weeks at a time. Everyone has their own unique family dynamic.

In my family, my brothers knew me and could irritate me beyond my ability to contain my anger and frustration. I would get so angry with them; I would throw things as well as say things I am sure if my mother heard I would be severely punished.

My mother had this saying, "If one person is laughing and the other is crying, it is not funny" Everything was "funny" between us, even my little brother's face while crying. Truly an ugly sight.

No matter how angry me and my siblings were, we would always find our way back to each other. I do not ever remember our bouts lasting more than an hour, other than the time in 1970 when I made my sister so angry that she threw a red patent leather platform shoe that landed right in the middle of my head! I vowed that she was out of my life forever.

Are you able to remember your very first real anger encounter and how it was handled?

Conflict resolution skills are learned very early in life. My sister's shoe-throwing taught her that hitting me worked. I cried, stopped aggravating her, and did not tell my parents. If my younger brother was asked, I am sure he could recall several occasions where I have thrown things and hit him too!

Controlling emotions is difficult in the heat of conflict, especially for children. My anger did not outweigh my love for my sister, we reconciled in the usual Travis fashion and just started talking again as if nothing happened.

I think it is also important to note I cannot remember what I did to make her so angry. I am sure I pushed until she, too, was extended beyond her capacity to hold her peace.

I deeply love my sister. I am not sure at that time I knew how much. Looking back, I believe if I did not love her, my anger could have led to bitterness and vindictive behavior that would have resulted in me returning the same shoe, different angle on a different day. Love motivated me to find internal resolve.

What happens when you are angry with someone you do not love or something you have no allegiance to? How do you find resolve? Have you been waiting for years for your "red shoe" opportunity?

I will confess... The skill my sister taught me when I was emotionally immature is still embedded in my psyche. I have witnessed that little girl in me surface on the highway and on the street! I do believe if pushed hard enough, the 8-year-old pushing, hitting, throwing Cheryl could fully appear.

What would the lord say about that Cheryl who is 53 but on occasion, is emotionally 8 years old?

2

ANGER'S PERFORMANCE

Psychology Today[1] says, "Anger is one of the basic human emotions, as elemental as happiness, sadness, anxiety, and disgust. These emotions are tied to basic survival and were honed over the long course of human history. Anger is related to the "fight, flight, or freeze" response of the sympathetic nervous system; it prepares humans to fight. But fighting doesn't necessarily mean throwing punches; it might motivate communities to combat injustice by changing laws or enforcing new behavioral norms. Of course, anger too easily or frequently mobilized can undermine relationships and it is deleterious to bodies in the long term. Prolonged-release of the stress hormones that accompany anger can destroy neurons in areas of the brain associated with judgment and short-term memory, and it can weaken the immune system."

Before studying to write this book, I knew that being angry could raise blood pressures but had no idea the extent of the impact anger has on our bodies. I had no idea that anger could literally make us sick in other ways or that Anger was such a hot topic.

The bible mentions anger more than 40 times. Did you know that the Lord gives us permission to be angry?

Ephesians 4:26 NASB

Be Angry and yet do not sin: do not let the sun
go down on your anger, and do not give
the devil an opportunity.

Anger is not a bad emotion. It is part of our human design. It is when anger performs and does not produce positive change that it becomes a problem.

Because I am aware that under the right circumstances, I could explode emotionally, I am on guard and challenge myself daily to control how far I allow myself to go. I now pray that the lord will control my mouth and emotions before I start my car. It may be just me, but shouting the word idiot from the inside of my car only leaves me feeling out of control and childish. It does not produce positive change. It is a fact that some people should not be on the road, they could easily hurt someone. My anger about the Bureau of Motor Vehicles giving a license to every driver that manages to pass the driver's test is not bad. The feeling of wanting to run them off the road? Bad. The National Highway Traffic Safety Administration[2] says that, "Fatal car crashes linked to aggressive driving climbed nearly 500% in 10 years!" I am the driver that may yell while inside my car but would never want to be confronted, sometimes fear is what motivates me to keep quiet and look straight ahead.

The Lord warns us not to sin because he knows that anger's performance can lead to sin. Protect yourself from people and things that provoke negative anger in you.

> **Matthew 7:6 AMP** *Do not give that which is*
> *holy to dogs, and do not throw*
> *your pearls before pigs, for they will*
> *trample them under their feet, and turn*
> *and tear you to pieces.*

People who challenge you to "Cast your pearls among the swine" with debates about politics and doctrine that are only meant to heat up your fight temperature. Discern and establish if these conversations are meant for productive communications or just to fulfill someone's need for a proverbial punching bag.

Be aware of friends who love drama, play victim, and look for you to rescue them from supposed injustice.

Beware of YouTube videos of vicious fights or arguments. Do you see yourself in the YouTube fight? Do you imagine what you would do or say in the place of the individual whose side you have chosen? I have been there and am transparent enough to tell the story.

If you find yourself watching these, being entertained and comfortable, heart check yourself. Pure hearts and clean hands do not feed themselves with bitter fights and arguments.

Giving the devil opportunity is what we must be careful of. The devil is a huge opportunist and takes advantage of every open door or crack to provoke you to anger. The bible says...

> **James 1:20 AMP**
> for the [resentful, deep-seated] anger of man
> does not produce the righteousness of God

[that standard of behavior which He
requires from us]

Deep-seated anger is not conducive to God-like behavior.

Anger that produces change, anger that provides safety, and anger that commands peace are all positive performances of anger. Anger that produces pain (physical or emotional), division, confusion, fear or bitterness is an example of anger's negative performance. Weigh that emotion when it comes. Take a couple of breaths and think about its source. Is your anger's performance negative or positive? Let's work on it.

ANGER THE INVISIBLE WALL

Anger should never cause you to be isolated from friends or family.

Have you removed yourself from communicating with family or friends? While it is always best to protect yourself from people who have a negative impact on your emotional wellbeing, be sure that you have not created an emotional wall because you are angry.

Are you aware of anger still festering over something that happened to you years ago? How many times have you told that story? Has that experience changed how much you trust or allow people into your life today? Are you impatient or easily irritated?

Search your heart for the source. It could be that your anger was initially caused because of your desire to set boundaries or to be safe. Maybe it began as positive anger.

The inability to resolve it for whatever reason has allowed it to remain and change its form into mistrust or bitterness. The bible says,

Ephesians 4:26
be angry and yet do not sin; do not let the sun
go down on your anger, and do not give the
devil an opportunity

The enemy is always waiting for a door, an opportunity to creep in while you are unaware and pervert good intentions. Pay close attention to how long this feeling lasts. It is ok if the anger shifts into righteous indignation. An example is in Matthew 21:12, when Jesus turned over the tables of the Money Changers in the temple. Because they were defiling the sacred temple.

Pay close attention to anger past "the sun going down on your wrath," next day anger or anger that lingers and turns into ruminating thoughts that control your day or night interrupting your sleep. Replaying the situation multiple times with role play and different responses. The thoughts that make you argue your point out loud when you are alone. Thoughts that bleed over into your conversations with others until you are repeating the problem to multiple people at different times. Becoming upset with people who are in no way attached to what caused you to be angry but because their behavior is reminiscent, you treat them as if they were the original cause of your anger. It's not OK to rekindle the emotion as if you are in the moment it happened. There is danger in those negative emotions becoming a part of how you interact with people, the decisions you make, your health and you may not even realize it.

A great way to give yourself a reality check is to think about how others view you. This may sound like a silly question, but do you have friends? What do most people say about you? Not what you think they say about you. Ask for honest, open feedback from a couple of people you trust and be ready to process it.

Are you often left off the list of invites, but assume it's an attack on you? Is it possible you are most often negative due to being angry about what happened to you? In conversation, for every positive comment, do you find yourself thinking of a negative in the name of playing the devil's advocate or "keeping it real/honest/one hundred?"

There is a scripture that says they judge themselves by themselves, commending themselves. Meaning the only measurement they use to determine if they are right in their thinking is their own intellect coupled with how great they think they are. They believe they are right and correct in everything based on their own greatness and not what the bible says.

I believe it is why we hear testimonies from convicts who tell stories of why they committed the crime and how they were justified based on their own view of the way things should be. It is appalling to listen to an offender explain how their victim, in some way, deserved to be a victim. Among a multitude of other issues, they are deranged in their thinking partly because their internal compass has no outside input.

> **2 Corinthians 10:12 AMP**
> *We do not have the audacity to put ourselves*
> *in the same class or compare ourselves*
> *with some who (supply testimonials to)*
> *commend themselves. When they measure*
> *themselves by themselves and compare*
> *themselves with themselves, they lack*
> *wisdom and behave like fools*

Let us invite sound opinions into our anger situations so that we are not left to ourselves to measure our own intellect by our intellect.

We are all learning continually and must be open to being educated by anyone or any circumstance. Even those whom we have deemed less informed.

My most powerful educational experience was through a child, unjaded by life-giving sound direction. It was a child that explained to me why I should never be afraid. The bible says in Isaiah 11:6, and a child shall lead them.

> **Proverbs 12:1 KJV**
> *Whoso loveth instruction loveth knowledge:*
> *but he that hateth reproof is brutish.*

4

ANGER THE BITTER TIMEOUT

In the second chapter of this book, we talked about a quote from Psychology Today "stress hormones that accompany anger can destroy neurons in areas of the brain associated with judgment."

Anger can stunt your ability to make sound decisions. We could be inadvertently giving ourselves a timeout for growth in decision making! Time is short. It takes time to recover from bad choices. The aftermath of Anger could be a thief of your time and money.

There was a time after my divorce, where I felt my time was wasted in the relationship. I was angry about that. The lord had to caution me so that I would not become bitter. The fact that I did not want to see my ex-husband prosper was a sign that I had resentment within.

As my healing began, I realized that there was not one moment I should regret in that marriage. I loved, I learned, and I grew.

Do not allow resentment to grow. The bible talks about a bitter root. Resentment taking root into the ground of your life can change your personality.

I love it when people describe me as being very sweet and mild-mannered. They are in disbelief when I am transparent about my past and present thoughts and behaviors.

Life changes us, and it should, but for good only. We should take our anger experiences and use them for positive change, teachable moments. We are human and need time to heal, we can certainly speed up that healing time if we look at our anger and hate experiences differently, and learn life lessons from them.

Resentment only produces contamination. It will even affect the grace of God on your life! Let me be clear... you can negatively affect God's favor and mercy towards you. Here is the scripture...

> **Hebrews 12:15 CJB**
> *See to it that no misses out on God's grace,*
> *that no root of bitterness springing up*
> *causes trouble and thus contaminates*
> *many,*

Do not be the bad apple that spoils the bunch and do not cause God to remove his favor from you. Anger is the conduit to unbecoming behaviors.

I have someone very close to me that has always displayed anger when I fall or injure myself. I have noticed that this person is that way with everyone he loves. He says things like, "I knew that was going to happen to you! You have got to be more careful!" I know now that it is just misplaced fear. As innocent as the cause is, the anger behavior is still damaging.

I am very sensitive to people who are considered outcasts because they are just plain mean. I have compassion because I know that somewhere in their life, they have felt wronged in some way and have not been able to resolve this emotion. Sometimes the resolve is forgiveness. The saying, "Forgive people for you, not for them" is correct. Forgiveness frees us from anger and resentment. It is also what the lord requires us to do for him to forgive us.

> **Matthew 6:15**
> *But if you do not forgive men their trespasses,*
> *neither will your Father forgive your*
> *trespasses.*

Forgiveness does not mean that you are letting a person get away with hurting you. Sometimes that is why it is so difficult to release and forgive. Work on letting the person deal with the consequences of hurting you without you seeing the punishment.

Because we are human, we like to see people pay for their wrong. Be willing to believe that our God's vengeance is more powerful than any punishment you can inflict. You will find that your punishment toward that individual hurts you more than anyone. Hate requires much more energy than love. It is not our job to punish.

> **Romans 12:19 AMP**
> *Beloved, never avenge yourselves, but leave*

the way open for God's wrath [and His judicial righteousness]; for it is written [in Scripture], "Vengeance is Mine, I will repay," says the Lord.

5

ANGER'S VICTIMS

There was a time that I was very angry at my ex-husband. I did not like him at all. I did not wish pain, but I certainly had a problem with him being happy based on thinking he did not deserve any good because of my then broken heart.

I remember a woman at my church trying to understand if I was separated from my husband why in the world was I sitting next to him in church and having conversations with him. She did not understand, nor did she like it.

In her mind, if we were separated, she thought there should be disdain or an enemy line that I should not cross. I did not explain my behavior because I did not understand it. I only knew that I loved him, and my love for him outweighed my desire to be mean or ugly toward him.

The lord had to continually remind me that as angry as I was with him, he still belonged to God. He was still his child and deserved to be treated kindly.

There were days I wanted to call him and give him all the hate I could muster. I am not implying that I was perfect. I am sure he has his own stories of my rolling eyes and hanging up on him.

I found as I grew, I was not angry at him at all. I was angry with God because my dream family was now broken. And even more angry that I had to accept some responsibility in the situation.

Anger settled and matured always has its victims, whether it is the woman cutting you off on the highway, the man cutting in front of you in the grocery store, or you believing you are hurting someone by isolating yourself.

I used to wonder how my mother could be so patient with people. There were mean girls even in the '60s and '70s in our neighborhood who would say mean things about my always quiet and kind mother. Today I still marvel at people's ability to stay calm when someone is pushing their buttons. I can speak for my mother and say that she lets things go. She does not allow it fester. Her compassion and love for people forces her into forgiveness mode. Matthew 5 says if you love only those who love you, what reward do you have?

My daily prayer includes asking God to help me to be more compassionate. To see people the way God sees them. The same way he sees me as his child flawed and ever learning.

6

ANGER'S KRYPTONITE

Love.

My mother has mastered the art of loving people. She has confessed to me on many occasions that she lacks scripture knowledge. I have said to her in those times, "But you live the scripture, Mom."

Do you know any of these people? They may not be able to quote scripture, but their love for God is evident in their behavior toward men.

I follow a modern-day Good Samaritan on social media. I watched a video of him at a grocery store shopping for a homeless family. When at the checkout line, he noticed that the loaf of bread he had chosen for the family was squashed. "Oh no! This bread is squashed; may I choose another one?" he asked the clerk. My heart swelled, and I cried. I was so moved by his care for these people he did not know, I also felt convicted.

Would I have noticed the squashed bread and chosen another loaf for the homeless person who, in my mind, may not care or have even noticed? My view before the video was that homeless people are thankful for whatever they can get, so second best or subpar should be fine.

My love for God's people should also include a desire for the very best for them. I had not realized until the moment he asked to exchange the bread how much work I still need in my love walk. John 15:17 *This I command you: that you love* and unselfishly seek the best for one another.

I have added yet another part to my daily prayer. God, please give me a heart for your people so that I will treat them as if I am in love with them the way you are in love with me. Please help me to love my neighbor as myself.

I have not arrived, but God loves us so much that he is ok with perfecting those things that concern us. We must love, without love, we have nothing.

> **1 Corinthians 13:2**
> *And though I have the gift of prophecy, and*
> *understand all mysteries and all*
> *knowledge, and though I have all faith, so*
> *that I could remove mountains, but have*
> *not love, I am nothing.*

And the ever-popular and most powerful scripture,

> **John 3:16**
> *For God so loved the world that he gave his*
> *only begotten son,*

Love kills all hate, anger, bitterness, and resentfulness. Love completely annihilates every negative emotion you could imagine. It is the antidote, remedy, and cure. The bible mentions love three hundred ten times!

After long periods, anger can change its form. My anger towards my husband turned into resentment. I did not want to see him prosper in any way. The thought of him being successful without me was excruciating. I did not want him to smile or enjoy life. I had to free myself from unforgiveness and stay in the lane of compassion. Understanding that although I may have my feelings about an individual, the lord wishes above all things that we prosper and be in good health even as our souls prosper, 3 John 2.

Who am I, and what authority do I have to wish anything different than what God desires for anyone? Even someone I may deem the worst person on earth. The lord still calls them his beloved.

Today, I am very proud to say that my ex-husband is my very best friend. The journey to arrive at this place included love, forgiveness, and compassion. This friendship would not be possible without love.

It may not always be evident that anger was the original source of your negative feelings about people, yourself, or about life in general. It is important to remember that Love is God's extinguisher for the burning fires of anger.

Find your way to love. Anger is a powerful emotion. God's love is stronger. Pray for God to forgive you, help you forgive and then ask him to increase your love for people, pray for him to give you a pure heart and clean hands. It's where I started!

7

SCRIPTURE HELP FOR ANGER

Proverbs 19:11 A man's discretion makes him slow to anger, And it is his glory to overlook a transgression.

Proverbs 22:24 Do not associate with a man given to anger; Or go with a hot-tempered man,

Proverbs 29:8 Scorners set a city aflame, But wise men turn away anger.

Proverbs 30:33 For the churning of milk produces butter, And pressing the nose brings forth blood; So the churning of anger produces strife.

Ecclesiastes 7:9 Do not be eager in your heart to be angry, For anger resides in the bosom of fools.

Ephesians 4:31 Let all bitterness and wrath and anger and clamor and slander be put away from you, along with all malice.

Colossians 3:8 But now you also, put them all aside: anger, wrath, malice, slander, and abusive speech from your mouth.

James 1:19 This you know, my beloved brethren. But everyone must be quick to hear, slow to speak and slow to anger;

Ephesians 4:26 NASB Be Angry and yet do not sin: do not let the sun go down on your anger, and do not give the devil an opportunity.

ENDNOTES

2. Anger's Performance

1. Psychology Today, Anger - https://www.psychologytoday.com/us/basics/anger
2. CNN, "Road rage is on the rise. Here's how to survive these dangerous encounters", September 10, 2019 - https://m.cnn.com/en/article/h_bb3b51839c83d1402bc32c2f98066a64

ABOUT THE AUTHOR

Cheryl M. Travis spends her days reviewing and investigating death claims for an insurance company in Columbus, Ohio. Because she loves what she does, Cheryl has over 30 years' experience communicating and advocating for the sick and grieving families. She is also a strong advocate for the Deaf and hard of hearing that began when her eldest child was diagnosed as profoundly deaf.

Cheryl surrendered her life to Christ in 1989. Her teaching ministry began in 1995 at Higher Ground Always Abounding Assemblies under the leadership of the Beloved and honorable Bishop Sherman S. Watkins.

Cheryl has two children Brice and Bailey, and in Nana bliss with one Grandchild Gavyn Marie Thomas.

She is currently a member of Rebirth Worship Center under the leadership of Apostle Darren Thomas, where she serves as an assistant Pastor. Her ministry focus is on assisting individuals with overcoming life obstacles through practical life application teaching while exposing the enemy and his devices to keep us bound and inactive.

It is Cheryl's life dream to live out her full purpose while on this earth, leaving no assignment undone.

facebook.com/cheryltravis.cunningham.3

twitter.com/cheryltc30

instagram.com/cheryl.travis

ALSO BY CHERYL TRAVIS

Help God, I Am Afraid

CPSIA information can be obtained
at www.ICGtesting.com
Printed in the USA
BVHW082157100121
597329BV00004B/14